VIC

Daughter   **Grandmother**

Queen   **Widow**

Wife **Mother**

Vera Morrill

Published by New Generation Publishing in 2014

Copyright © Vera Morrill 2014

First Edition

www.newgeneration-publishing.com

New Generation Publishing

About the Author

VERA MORRILL. Formerly an English teacher, she holds an Hons. Degree from Southampton University and was an English Examiner on the Cambridge University Examination Board. She is a Licentiate of the London Academy of Music and Dramatic Art, with a Teaching Diploma for Speech and Drama and a Gold Medal for acting. She has written and broadcast stories for the BBC, scripted and produced theatrical productions and is a published poet.

Her work includes:-

Tales of the Isle of Wight
A Formidable Fortune
Beginners Please
Retribution
The Ann Hathaway Diaries
The Queen's Neighbours
Life on the Edge

.....

Sketches by Lynne Phillips

Victoria

Victoria's Adolescence	Born 1819
The future unveiled	
Suspicions	
Victoria Regina	1837 Accession 18 years of age
June 20th 1837	Meets Privy Councillors
My Daily Life	
Pageantry & the Aftermath	1838 Coronation
Lady Flora Hastings	1839
The Proposal	1839
Our Very Royal Wedding	1840
Married Life	
Our Love	
Pregnancy	1840 Princess Royal born, November
My Children	
Attacker's Target	1st Attack 1840
Isle of Wight Revisited	
Beautiful Osborne	1845/46
Finding Balmoral	1848
The Great Exhibition	1851
The Crimean War	1854
Albert's Title	
Empress of India	1859
Albert's Death	1861
John Brown's Death	1883
My Munshi	1887
Dear, Desolate Osborne	
My Last message	
Victoria, Grandmother of Europe	

…..

Photograph of the young Queen Victoria in her coronation robes, courtesy of the Isle of Wight County Press.

Victoria's life was one of joys and sorrows. Her love of Albert so intense that it survived early marital disagreements. His death, leaving her a widow at forty-two with nine children, left her so distraught that for a time doctors thought it might affect her brain. There were eight attempts to harm her, some by the mentally unstable. Her close friendship with John Brown was ridiculed and his death too, left her desolate. Years later her kindness towards the young Indian, Abdul Karim, was scorned by the public and her own children. She loved painting and writing and here I have tried to set down her own words, how she herself might have regarded her multitude of experiences. All the experiences are based on fact and on the proven data regarding her reaction to them.

Victoria's Adolescence

Laughter rarely features in my life
Mama hardly ever smiles,
Meeting girls my own age
Never an option.
Then came the day,
The amazing day,
My laughter refused to be silent
And pealed out,
Shattering the quietude.

Mama recoiled in horror
Why was I so amused?
Laughter, so very unladylike!
It seemed, today had been chosen
To convey to me new knowledge.
No longer an infant,
I was to learn that, unbelievable,
I was the bearer of blue blood.

Ignoring Mama's face,
Frosty, disconcerted,
I continued to chuckle,
Found it uncontrollably funny.
Blue blood in my veins?
I know only too well its colour,
The brightest red
In common with everyone around me!

Scowling, Mama left the room
Calling to Lehzen to join her.
As they left, I heard the words,
'Tomorrow, she will not be amused'.

…..

Victoria in her teens

Footnote: Victoria's mother was the widowed Duchess of Kent. By birth a Saxe Coburg, she was increasingly aware, as her late husband's brothers became older and without heirs apparent, of Victoria's proximity to the throne.

The Duchess of Kent was a difficult lady. German by birth, she was not popular with the staff, the Royals, or with the English people. Rarely did Victoria see other children. Only Baroness Lehzen, Victoria's governess was very close to Victoria and ensured that the girl was prepared for what might lie ahead.

Duchess of Kent

The Future Unveiled

My history lessons with Lehzen
Have taught me well.
I know that here, for several years
There has been a succession of elder sons,
Some of questionable ability.
Then at last, in 1830, came my uncle,
The new King, William the Fourth.

My teacher knew I was fond of him
And that the fondness was reciprocated.
His own two girls had both been lost
In their infancy.
Always he seemed to enjoy my company,
Told me I was intelligent
And that he liked my enthusiasm.
Adding that I was too repressed,
Required more outlet for my spirit,
This obviously a dig at Mama,
Whose presence he always resents.

The next day, without comment,
Lehzen placed on my desk,
A genealogy chart.
I studied its contents,
Sensing my teacher's silent tension.
At last I turned to her
Eyes wide open,
'This suggests I am to become Queen.
But surely not, Lehzen?'
'It is certain, Victoria.'

'But the King, my dear Uncle,
He may live for years yet',
'Your Uncle, the King, is, I am afraid,
No longer young. You must be prepared.'

And, seeing my horror,
At the enormity of it all,
'Do not be alarmed.
We will ensure that you are ready.
You are not alone, Victoria.'

At last, the shock absorbed,
I began to think it through,
Followed the lines with my pen.
Now I saw quite clearly,
My position in line to the throne
And it was very close.

I tried to absorb the enormity of it all.
And, still unsure, again turned to Lehzen,
'So... it is I, who will follow now.
It is I who will be Queen?'
'Yes, Victoria, it is you!'

Carefully, I brushed back
A strand of unruly hair.
Opened my exercise book
And, after smiling up at her,
Wrote with a flourish,
'Victoria Regina'.

.....

Footnote: Baroness Lehzen was a German. Since
            Victoria's childhood, Lehzen, as she was
            known, had been her personal attendant
            and Governess.

            Lehzen ensured that Victoria was made aware of the
            problems ahead.

4

Suspicions

Mama's close association with Sir J Conroy
Has worried me for some time.
I don't like the man!
One day he is all smiles
And honeyed conversation.
The next, he is overtly critical
And acid-tongued.

It has taken me some time
But now I am sure of his intentions.
When I become Queen
He wishes Mama to be appointed my regent
He would then bend Mama to his wishes
And thus be in a position of supreme control.

I could never agree to this
And pray that I may reach an age
To be accepted by the Council
Without the necessity of a Regent.

．．．．．

Footnote: Sir John Conroy was disliked by many at the court.
On one occasion he asked Victoria to sign some
papers, but realising his intentions were to ensure
should she become Queen, he would then make her
mother, the Duchess of Kent, her Regent, thus
giving himself a great deal of power, to his
annoyance and anger, Victoria refused!!

Victoria Regina

They arrived at dawn
Elder statesmen, grey-faced
Wearied with age and duty.
Roused from my sleep
I entered the room and,
Whey-faced, surveyed the scene,
Saw the subservient bowed heads
Heard the words 'Your Majesty'
And knew…
I was Queen.

The expected tears unshed
Fears for what lay ahead unspoken,
More composed than they
I listened carefully
And understood.
Inbred inhibitions fell away
Decisions must be made
Decisions I alone could make…
I was Queen.

Mama and my Governess in the shadows
And there must remain
This now is *my* life, *my* people, *my* domain…
I am Queen.

June 20th 1837

I had not known, could not have known
It would be like this.
Sorrowing at the loss of my beloved uncle,
Overwhelmed at the suddenness of bows
And curtsies and, most of all, the repetitive,
'Your Majesty' 'Your Grace'.
It had all come true
I really am the Queen of England.

Now, dressed in black,
I enter the Council Chamber
Wait as the elderly Privy Councillors
Stand, heads bowed.
Until I reach the head of the table.
A few deep breaths and I am ready to speak,
To ask for their consideration and support
As I undertake this awesome task.
They remain standing for my departure,
Heads bowed again and it is over.

Good news followed, via Mama.
The dear old Duke of Wellington had told her
My voice had been clear as a bell.
Expressing astonishment at my composure,
He added, "Had it been one of my own daughters
Speaking, I could not have been more proud."

There was bad news too, for Mama!
Her rule since my childhood that, always,
I must be escorted up and down stairs,
I have put an end to that.
The idea that she must share my bedroom
I have also brought to a halt.
Informing her that these occurrences
Would appear ridiculous to others

And that sleeping arrangements for me
Are already being prepared elsewhere.
Reluctantly, but with no other course,
She has had to accept.

Now, at last, I can retire in privacy.
This day started in the morning's early hours
It has been long and required much of me.
I pray that my dear Uncle may rest in peace.
And that God will watch over me
During the days to come,
As I attempt to fulfil my new and demanding role.
With His help I will find the strength
To do all that is expected of me.

.....

Footnote: Victoria had been roused from her sleep in the early
            hours. Only when she saw the statesmen's bowing
            and heard the words 'Your Majesty' did she realise
            she was Queen of England.

            Later in the day she had to greet the Privy
            Councillors, in addition to asking for their assistance
            and support in her new role as Queen of England.
            Finally she was able to pray for her lost Uncle and
            ask for God's help in finding strength in the days to
            come.

            Victoria's resolution was, for an eighteen year old
            amazing. In the years to come, she was to show that
            same sense of power, occasionally defying others,
            with her outstanding sense of authority.

My Daily Life

A pattern to my new life now emerges,
Bathed and dressed,
Breakfast eaten and I am ready.
Dear Lehzen always at my side
As paperwork is passed to me,
Signed and handed back,
My diary checked,
Additions entered.

Then came the letters
And photographs...
New challenges to add to my list
A whole raft of European princes
Suddenly aware of my existence
Expressing the pleasure
It would give them
To make my acquaintance.
Hard on the heels of those letters,
Others giving detailed outlines
Of the princes' individual charms,
Their love of music and art.
At the arrival of the fifth letter
Lehzen and I collapsed in giggles.
Impossible to live up to the standard
Of these god-like creatures.

Another letter, from Hanover,
My Coburg cousins, Albert and Ernest,
Send their congratulations
Ask if it would be possible for them to visit.
At last, people I've already met,
Albeit some time ago,
People nearer my own age
With whom I can relax.

My welcome is sincere,
A light in the darkness

.....

Footnote: Very soon other European princes were asking for
permission to visit the new Queen, but at last were
two cousins she had met before, the Princes Albert
and Ernest from Coburg.

This delighted her, Victoria has met and enjoyed
their company – sons of Leopold, King of the
Belgians.

Inundated by the many requests to meet the young
Queen, with Lehzen's help Victoria declined many,
but was determined to see again her Coburg friends.
Already she has been aware of Prince Albert's
handsome figure, his charm and kind manner.

She was beginning to think he was the one!!

Pageantry & the Aftermath

My coronation,
A breathtaking experience.
The weight of the crown,
The chanting of the peers of the realm
And outside…
The noise and cheerfulness of the crowds
All music to my ears.

The people don't seem to mind my youth,
Rather they seem to embrace it.
Perhaps they are tired of elderly kings.
They have given me much to think about.
Lehzen has told me a great deal
About the poverty that exists
And the resultant diseases.
I have already expressed my concern.
The Prime Minister sought to brush it aside,
Thought me exaggerating
But I have made it clear,
I intend to see some changes.

My move to Buckingham Palace
Took place with ease.
So much is possible when money
And a vast number of servants are available.
Mama's friend will not be here,
She is not happy about it,
But to have Conroy living in my house
Would be beyond the pale
His constant visits irksome.
If they wish to meet,
They must do so elsewhere

Here I have Ladies in Waiting,
Which sounds very grand.
From one I learned Conroy is unpopular.

Certainly his behaviour is what resulted
In my dear late Uncle William's inability
To tolerate Mama's company.

I have so much to learn,
My life has been turned upside down.
Lehzen is saying it is time to retire,
But how can I sleep?
My head is ringing with the sights and sounds
Of this amazing day…
I, Victoria, am Queen!!

…..

Footnote: Victoria was clearly delighted at the pageantry of the coronation. The weight of the crown was daunting but she had been well versed by Lehzen and once they were in Buckingham Palace she was able to see the number of Ladies in Waiting ready for her pleasure and assistance.

Victoria was fortunate that her first Prime Minister, Lord Melbourne, was an excellent teacher. From him she learned the principles of the constitution and understood her own prerogative, i.e. what, in her own right she was entitled to do. Letters Patent allowed her to make certain decisions. She was able to do this when precedence said that at the changeover of parties and Prime Ministers she should find a new set of ladies in waiting. This, to the consternation of ministers, she refused to do.

Lady Flora Hastings

Disaster struck yesterday!
Whilst at Kensington Palace
I formed a dislike for Flora Hastings.
Repeatedly Mama seemed to delight
In making her join Lehzen and me,
As if to ensure confidences between us
Would be overheard
And, presumably, passed on.
I hated these situations.
The girl is too friendly with Mama
And perhaps, more especially
With Conroy, whom I detest.

Following my accession
And the move to Buckingham Palace
I have my own new posse of Ladies in Waiting.
But yesterday, when a replacement was needed
Who should appear but Lady Flora?
She had put on weight!
To me, during the next few days,
And noted by others,
The expansion round her middle
Had started to enlarge.
She is unmarried,
But there seems little doubt…
She is with child!!

On my instructions
Lady Portman dismissed her from Court
And, I was informed,
Flora left in floods of tears.
In a short while, a second blow struck,
Refusing to see our Court doctor,
She employed a physician
Who had known her since birth,

He was given permission
To perform an intimate examination and…
She was found to be a virgin!

Further, even more humiliating,
A tumour in her abdomen was discovered.
My own embarrassment knows no bounds
And the repercussions are proving
Both unexpected and unpleasant
Although apologies have been made
And, on the face of it, accepted,
The news has spread.

When out in my carriage,
I am now finding the journey unpleasant
Onlookers turn their backs as we approach,
Others start to boo,
Or even raise clenched fists
In my direction.
Most disconcerting!!

....

Footnote: Lady Flora's surgeon proves there is no suspicion of pregnancy, but that the problem is a tumour in her abdomen.

At one point, Lady Flora Hastings' aristocratic family, were so incensed by the suggestion about their daughter that they discussed legal action, against the Royal household. Fortunately they decided against this.

Victoria was to learn that her people had sometimes to be handled with care.

The Proposal

He is handsome, manly,
Intelligent
Impressively elegant,
Impeccably courteous,
Steeped in protocol
But with a quiet sense of humour
And a twinkle in his eyes.
In short, he is perfect!

Discarded now the fulsome letters,
The photos of a raft of princes,
Blue blooded, solemn faced,
I need look no further,
My search is done.
He is the one.

But, here's the rub…
It is I must ask the question
Subdue my palpitations and
Fractured nerves,
Stifle the mayhem around
My quaking heart.

Supposing, heaven forbid,
Fearful of the commitment,
Overawed by the years ahead
He should say no.
Imagine the shock waves,
The shame, a queen declined,
My heart broken.

He has arrived!
Courteously he bows his head
"Your Majesty".
Am I trembling? Blushing?

I sit down, gesturing to him,
A courteous acknowledgement
And he sits beside me.

But… how to start?
Where to start? Then, hesitating,
"Albert… Would you, could you?
Do me the supreme honour of becoming
My husband?"
"Your Majesty, my Darling Victoria,
I will be both honoured and delighted."
Leaning forward
He takes me in his arms
And, oh, what rapture!... kisses me.

This is the beginning…
The fragility of our unspoken love
Strengthened, given purpose
Now we may face the future together.
I was right, Albert,
Dear, dear Albert, loves me
Not for my royal blood,
Not for my throne,
But for myself alone.
Receded, all my fears
I am wanted, needed.

Hand in hand, we leave the room,
Our smiles speak volumes
And the assembled company,
Delights in our joy.

…..

Footnote: As Queen, Victoria, and not the male, must make the
proposal of marriage. Her delight in Albert's
acceptance was evident from the start. In spite of the

public's reluctance to accept a German prince, he proved to be her rock and mainstay. Her tendency to obstinacy and stubbornness as a child continued and Albert was the only person in her life at this time, who was able to reason with her and make her see sense. She had fallen in love with him from the start and although at first it was felt he was merely fulfilling the wishes of his father, that he marry the young English Queen, they became together a loving and caring couple – albeit with the inevitable quarrels and disagreements!

Our Very Royal Wedding

Here in this holy place
Amidst pomp and circumstance sublime
Our love shines forth
Envelops all,
This is our time.

We cherish the ritual unfolding
Precious keepsakes for our future.
Family and friends
And untold millions
Wish us well.
This is our time
To enjoy and remember always.

This poem is for you, my Dearest Albert,
In an attempt to express my devotion
And my daily thank you prayers
For having been blessed
With such a wonderful husband.

.....

Footnote: Victoria and Albert's Royal Wedding took place at
1.0p.m., on the 10th February at the Chapel Royal,
St. James.

The weather was dreadful with torrents of rain and
violent gusts of wind. Hundreds of people still
thronged the park in spite of this. Later, the day
cleared and the sun gave way to what became
known as 'Queen's weather'.

Victoria left Buckingham Palace accompanied by
the Duchess of Kent and the Mistress of the
Robes. The young Queen wearing a white satin
gown with a deep flounce of Honiton lace, a
diamond necklace and ear-rings and the magnificent
sapphire brooch, Albert's gift to her.

Her 12 young train-bearers wore white with white roses. As the Queen entered the chapel there was a flourish of trumpets.

Given away by her uncle, the Prince wore the uniform of the British Army with the order of the Garter.

Lord Melbourne later assured her 'Nothing could have gone off better'.

Albert proved to be not only a kind and devoted husband, but also intelligent and skilful. He carefully ensured that in Buckingham Palace and Windsor Castle, all toilets in the Royal households were brought up to date.

Later he provided a private building for Victoria, so that she could cope with her letters and sit and watch the sea. When the children were old enough, the Swiss Chalet was built where they could play and later sail with Albert. Always, the Queen would wave to them from the beach, a joy to them all.

Married Life

Lehzen had ensured I was well-versed
In the rites of marriage.
Books had been produced
On the art of coupling and procreation.
Museums displaying nude statues
Of both genders visited
Information conveyed that for some women
Activity in the marital bed
Had proved both horrifying and distressing.
I do not fall into that category!!

Albert, my dear, dear Albert
Is both tender and loving.
The absence of demonstrations of affection
In my childhood and adolescence
Mean that, to me, the warmth of his caresses
Are rapture to my soul.
Deo gratias.

Our Love
A poem for you alone, Albert

Knows no parameters
No territory where it may not tread
A jewel roughly hewn in youth's illusions,
Crude in its innocence
Raw in its naivety
We seized it with both hands
And shaped it together
Tempered its form with humour and sensitivity
Guarded its vulnerability.
Now, honed by treasured memories
Shared sorrows and pleasures
The patina of the years reflects
Its many-faceted perfection.

Pregnancy

Yes, there was rejoicing at my pregnancy
A Queen's primary duty, it seems,
Is to produce a male heir to the throne.
Whilst my infant Victoria's birth
Did not meet that requirement
It was, for Albert and for me
A shared delight.

But then, of necessity,
A son must be born
And as the years pass
Our family grows and grows.
Now, daily, I give thanks for nannies,
Unaware of the attention children required.
Albert was from the start
More ready and indeed more able
In the art of parenthood.
He is, for me and for them
Our rock and constant source of joy.

.....

Footnote: In the early stages of Victoria's nine pregnancies
there was no gas to alleviate pain and Victoria
seemed to find little joy in the new arrivals. Not
until they were all much older did she seem to
become close to them. Perhaps some of her own
mother's genes resulted in her finding close affinity
with her children difficult?

My Children

Constantly I ask myself
Why have my children
Not brought me pleasure?
Our first child, Vicky,
Was from the start, devoted to her father
Inevitably my other commitments,
Often resulted in my exclusion,
So, she became closer to him than to me,
Albert, I accept, finds it easier than I
To be with young children.
I blame this on the fact
That, as a child,
I so rarely played with others.

From the start, dear Albert and I
Were in agreement.
Our family should set an example
Of monarchy at its best.
Sadly, this is not so easily achieved.
We ensure that the nannies are aware
Of the regimen required
For all our offspring,
But still we find ourselves failing.

Our two eldest sons, Bertie and Alfred
Are proving a great disappointment.
Sadly, in spite of lectures
And reprimands
They both now seem set on a course
Of frivolity,
Without serious purpose or interest.

Arthur, our third son,
At least seems to toe the line
He performs well in his cadet group
But I worry that once he goes to sea
He, too, might fall by the wayside.

My task, very soon,
Will be to find them suitable partners
To this end I regularly survey
European genealogy charts.
I must ensure that each child
Marries well and passes my bloodline
Into children of the coupling.
With, of course, the exception
Of Leo.

Only Leo, our dear invalid,
Without complaint,
Suffers his haemophilia,
Seems to accept my regulations,
Knowing that they always are given
With his interests at heart.
Albert's news,
That two members of his family

Had died from the disease
Was a terrible shock
But I was resolute,
Leo would be guarded well.
He dislikes not spending more time
With the family
But this surely protects him
From boisterous fun
And the possibility of accidents?
Yes, I protect him
If that means cosseting the dear boy,
So be it.

There is little doubt
I am not maternal by nature.
I am prepared to admit
To myself alone,
That whilst the act of procreation
Is loving and caring,
The aftermath of climax,
Is serious anti-climax.

.....

Attacker's Target

I never saw myself as a possible victim
Until the first occasion.
Albert and I were taking the air
When he saw a man standing at the kerbside
Suddenly draw from his coat pocket
A gun, aimed at our carriage.
My dear one, threw himself across my body
As others on the pavement rushed forward.
They caught hold of the man,
Police ran to help
And the man was taken away.

This was the forerunner
Of several similar instances
And by attackers of the same mould
All seemingly mentally unstable,
Homeless, poverty stricken,
Or in some way delusional.
In several cases the gun used
Was unloaded, or even artificial,
This knowledge, is of course,
Of little use when it is pointing at you!

Suddenly a man leapt from the crowd
Climbed up my side of the carriage
And started to hit me with his cane
Only the stiff rim of my bonnet
Saved me from serious injury
Even so, I had a black eye,
A cut on the forehead, severe bruises
And a devastating headache
For some time afterwards.

My greatest distress was not for my injuries
But that my children, with me in the carriage,

Should have witnessed such a dreadful thing.
Dear Albert was devastated
That this should have happened
When he was not able to protect us.

The one thing that came out of this
Was that, suddenly, my own and Albert's popularity
Took a turn for the better
It was as though my people were anxious
For our protection.
Suddenly the world did not seem so bleak.

…..

Footnote: Between 1840 and 1882, there were seven attacks on Queen Victoria by men and youths. Some of those involved were mentally unstable, one was sent to Bedlam and others, several of whom were found to have unloaded pistols, were punished by transportation. Parliament then changed the law so that threatening the monarch was made an imprisonable offence to be punished by flogging and culprits would not preen themselves in notoriety, but be disgraced.

Isle of Wight Revisited

When I was twelve years old,
Mama and I visited the Isle of Wight.
We stayed in an old castle,
Norris Castle,
And daily we went for walks.
I remember seeing Osborne House
And after our wedding telling Albert
Of how I was drawn to its situation
So close to the sea.
We went to see it together
And here Albert's intelligence
Came to the fore.
He quickly drew a sketch
Showing how the house could be enlarged
And turned into a small palace.
I was enchanted,
Our own home with gardens
And lands rolling down to the sea.
Complete privacy
Where the children could play in safety,
In fact, a perfect family home!

…..

Beautiful Osborne

To say I loved Osborne
Is an understatement.
There for the first time
I grew closer to my children
Helping Lady Lyttleton
(In charge of the nursery)
And the children's governess.
I assisted with bath-times,
Kissed the children when they were good
And spanked them when naughty.

Occasionally,
We would pick fruit together
In the Island's lovely climate,
Raspberries and strawberries.
If the children wished to sail
With their Papa
We agreed a position on the shore
Where I could see their approach
And we would wave to each other.

Whenever possible,
Breakfast, lunch and tea
Were taken outdoors
Under the lawn's magnificent cypress tree.
Or, in a retreat, dear Albert
Had designed for me.
It is close to the shore
And its mosaic floor
And ceiling of pink, blue and marigold
Create such a warm and inviting atmosphere.
There I can happily work at my papers,
Sketch, relax or read,
Sometimes just happy to enjoy the view.

It was at Osborne
I bathed in the sea for the first time.
A bathing machine was prepared
Taken down to the water's edge
And I would enter from the beach side.
Then aided, change into my bathing dress
Exiting through the side
Where the steps took me down into the sea.
Nervous at first,
I then found it quite delightful.
The water was warm
And so relaxing.

Close to the sea is the Swiss chalet.
I had asked Albert if a small house
For the children was possible.
As always, he was meticulous
In his planning.
The result was delightful.
A Swiss type chalet with a kitchen
Where the children can cook
And invite Albert and me to tea!
Gardens designed for their playing,
A vegetable area where they can learn

To plant seed and watch it grow.
They love it!!

.....

Footnote: Osborne House is open to the public for a large part of
the year. The beautiful gardens are designed to reflect
the Victorian age. In the house are magnificent
paintings by Winterhalter of the Royal family, the
nursery and a wealth of memorabilia related to
Victoria and Albert. It is possible to ride by carriage
down the lane to the Swiss Chalet created by Albert
for the children and to see the Queen's bathing
machine.

Osborne is still today known for Prince Albert's
passion for his garden design and carefully trimmed
pathways. Visitors enjoy seeing there, the wealth of
flowers and variety of plants.

Known too, is Queen Victoria's love of flowers and
how she always liked her home to have arrangements
there, from Albert's walled garden.

Finding Balmoral

I had hoped… believed
That in Osborne, we had found
The oasis of complete privacy,
Which, we, as a family, all needed.
Then, that dream was shattered.
Several incidents occurred,
Which made us realise
Intruders know no bounds.

The alarm was first raised
When one morning the children said
They had seen two people
Walking in the park.
Next, one of the servants,
Saw someone on our beach.
The police were informed
And daily patrols were arranged.

Suddenly, one afternoon,
Albert himself was confronted
Not by an intruder, but by a policeman
Who told him in no uncertain terms
That he was trespassing on private property.
He allowed himself to be taken to the house
And, it was as they entered the kitchen
And everyone rushed to stand up and bow
That the policeman realised the man
Whose arm he was holding,
Was the Prince!
Afterwards we could laugh about it,
Albert congratulated the man on his thoroughness,
(Which he had been testing)
Insisting that he stay and take a drink with us.

A train service is now available
From London to the South Coast,
So transit to Portsmouth
And from there to the Isle of Wight
Is fairly easy for anyone with evil intentions.

We now feel a further family home
Is needed, one defying intrusion,
Somewhere, a long way from London.
On the royal yacht, Albert and I
Started to travel North, searching
Different areas and buildings
In Scotland.
Until at last, we found Balmoral.
Its backdrop of highlands,
Compactness and homely feeling,
Was, we felt, just what we needed.
For us, it was perfect!

.....

The Great Exhibition 1851

Albert has dreamed of this moment
For many months.
There were hurdles to overcome,
The Government refused money,
But my amazing husband continued his work,
Approached the richest of supporters
Visited locally, trades' sites and factories,
Contacted firms all over the world
Ensuring that anything on show
Would be both impressive and perfect.

Joseph Paxton was, from the start, his rock.
Having seen Paxton's work at a mansion house
Albert had complete faith in his scientific
Knowledge and creativity.
His suggestions for building a Crystal Palace
Of glass and metal,
Covering many acres of Hyde Park
Delighted dear Albert.
The gloom and doom of bad omens
Were brushed aside.

They were told panes of glass
Would break under heavy rainfall,
Strong sunlight would make the interior
Uninhabitable.
Unshakeable, they persisted,
Albert's faith in Paxton's ability remained.
The three great elms left standing,
Around which the building was created.
Gave cause for thought.
Birds still nested there and our dear old friend,
The Duke of Wellington was asked
What can be done?
'Get a Sparrow Hawk Ma'am'.
They did so and the problem was solved.

At last the longed for day.
Above us the 3-tiered brilliance of crystal
In its framework of light blue
With touches of orange and scarlet,
Carrying the flags of all nations.

A fanfare of trumpets and we enter,
Albert holding the hand of Vicky
And I, that of the Prince of Wales.
We move to the chairs prepared for us
But do not sit.
Before us the exquisite crystal fountain.
The National Anthem first, then,
A short blessing from the Archbishop
Followed by the swell of the enormous organ
And 200 musicians, together with 600 voices
Singing the Alleluia Chorus.
Next comes the royal procession down the Nave,
Returning to our places at Albert's signal
To Lord Breadalbane. Once there, his Lordship
Said in a loud voice 'Her Majesty commands
Me to declare the Exhibition opened'.
This followed by a flourish of trumpets,
And much cheering.

Our eventual return to Buckingham Palace
Saw us replete with exclamations of wonder
And delight at the perfection of the opening
And the wondrous exhibits there for all to see.
My own joy is overflowing that at last,
My dear, dear Albert will now be recognised
For his intellect and creativity.
I am richly blessed.

.....

Footnote: The Prince's aim to promote human industry & skill, meant many different nations contributed. More than 6 million people visited the Exhibition between 1st May & October 15, 1851

Footnote: The Great Exhibition. Opening of the Crystal Palace

The Crimean War

The sudden realisation by my generals
That Russia was making inroads into Turkey
With the probable intention of seizing the country
And gaining complete control over the Black Sea,
Resulted in an unexpected unity between
France and ourselves.
Together our armies moved to the area
To try and prevent this happening.
It proved to be a war which took its toll
On our young men.
In addition to the warfare,
Many were killed by the cruel cold
And by disease. Cholera was rife.
As a country we are shamed
By the mismanagement which occurred.
Foodstuffs and clothing for the army,
Medical supplies were all on ships
Six miles away in the harbour.
A harbour which was an impassable
Sea of mud.

Buildings to which the wounded were taken
Were dirty beyond belief.
Had it not been for the arrival
Of a young woman called Florence Nightingale,
Enterprising beyond belief
Ruling her staff with a rod of iron,
Demanding and getting a measure of
Cleanliness, then more lives would have been lost.

One serious error followed another.
Our Light Brigade was ordered into a valley
On each side of which were the Russian guns,
Making them easy targets
Many brave soldiers died.
The poet, Mr Tennyson, so incensed by the phrase

In 'The Times', which informed its readers that
'Someone had blundered',
Included the phrase in a poem
Describing the Brigade's ride into the valley
And the disastrous consequences.

At the end of the war I went to the Marble Hall
Where I was to meet, just returned from abroad,
Thirty-two of the Grenadier Guards.
So many had lost limbs…
I was so overcome that my speech,
For the first time, could not be made.
The words just stuck in my throat
And I had to indicate to their Colonel
That he should tell them
All would soon get their richly deserved medals.

.....

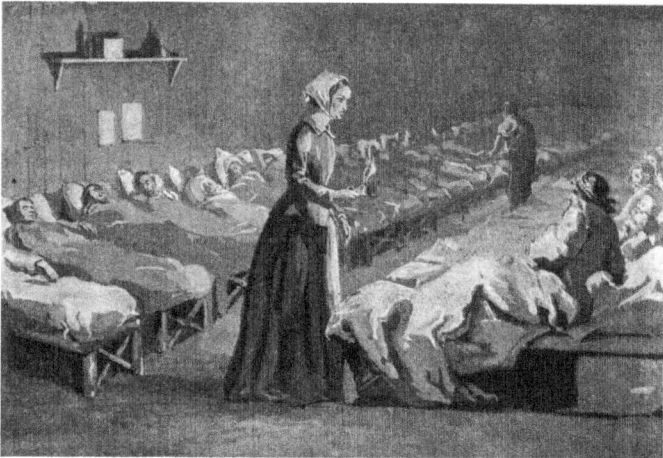

Footnote: The Queen's shock at seeing these young wounded men and learning of their bravery resulted in the creation of the Victoria Cross. The 26th June 1857 saw the first distribution of these. It was awarded to all ranks, private soldiers, commissioned ranks and non-commissioned officers, in the Navy as well as the Army.

Inscribed 'For Valour' it is given only to men who have served in the presence of the enemy and performed some single act of bravery or devotion.

In 1857 it carried with it a pension of £10.00 a year.

Seating for 12,000 people was erected in Hyde Park, 4,000 troops were present and it was estimated 100,000 people were in the park.

The Queen mounted, with the Prince Consort and Prince Frederick of Prussia, personally decorated 62 men. Each was brought to her and she bent from her horse to pin the cross on his breast.

As each man withdrew, Prince Albert bowed to mark his own respect.

Albert's Title

Repeatedly, ever since we were married,
I have asked that Albert be given the title
Of Prince Consort.
Always the Government has refused to do so.
With the marriage of our daughter,
The Princess Royal to Prince Fritz
Of Prussia, imminent,
Without the title of Consort
I foresaw difficulties.
My dear one, would,
In the order of precedence
Have to follow his son,
The Prince Regent, Bertie,
Albert could also be preceded
By royal guests at the wedding.
I could not bear the thought of this.
Once again I scoured documentation
Relating to our predicament.

After reading the Cabinet minutes
I discussed the situation
At length with Lord Palmerston,
Expressing the opinion that
It would surely be possible,
Quicker and without creating
Further complications to the monarchy
If I were to give Albert the tile 'Consort'
As is my prerogative, by Letters Patent.
It was immediately agreed
And Albert's new title inserted into the prayers
Said for the royal family.

I feel aggrieved that my advisers
Have not previously suggested this
As an alternative to the long discussions

And regular refusals by Parliament.
Now I can concentrate on my dear girl's wedding
And ensure that her trousseau and wardrobe
Is the envy of a multitude of German royal
Aunts and cousins.

.....

Footnote: The Princess Royal was 17 in November 1857 and married Prince Frederick William on 25th January 1858. Her wedding dress was of white moiré antique, trimmed with flounces of Honiton lace embroidered with sprays and wreaths of orange flowers and myrtle, with a matching veil and wreath to match.

Queen Victoria wore mauve and silver moiré antique, trimmed with Honiton lace, Her train was velvet, also trimmed with lace and she wore the royal diadem and the crown diamonds.

In the bridal procession, the Princess Royal walked between her father, the Prince Consort and the King of the Belgians, preceded by the elder three of her sisters.

The bride's grandmother, the Duchess of Kent wore purple velvet trimmed with ermine.

Prior to the bridal couple's departure for Prussia, Prince Frederick, known as Fritz, was invested with the Order of the Garter.

Within a short while after her marriage, Vicky was pregnant. Her labour was difficult and Queen Victoria's first grandchild was born with a dislocated left arm. He was christened William and later became known in the U.K. as Kaiser Bill.

Empress of India

My first encounter with Mr Disraeli
Was not auspicious.
I found those black, rather oily
Curls and flamboyant dress
Quite unsuitable for a member
Of my government.

However, further acquaintance
Enabled me to look beyond
His unusual appearance
And to concentrate on the man himself.
(Albert often chastises me, quite rightly,
For being too set in my ways!)

I now find Mr Disraeli to be a man
Of greater depth than I imagined.
He is married and obviously
Devoted to his wife.
Charming and informative
To my children
And always helpful should he think
I have a concern

And I did have a concern
On realising that Bertie had gone to India,
Without informing me in advance
And certainly, without my permission.
India has always been a source
Of fascination.
Such a vast country with its handsome
Coloured people, different religions
And a multitude of wild animals.
How I personally would have loved
To go there.

I was expressing all this to Mr Disraeli
And he listened most carefully
And then said, "I think Ma'am,
It is time that you were appointed
Empress of India."
My delight knew no bounds
And now I have a new title,
A very precious title.

…..

Footnote: The Queen learned that Mr Disraeli loved
              primroses. He enthused about seeing the Island in
              the Spring when the primroses were in bloom and
              on his death her gift sent to the undertakers was a
              basket of primroses.

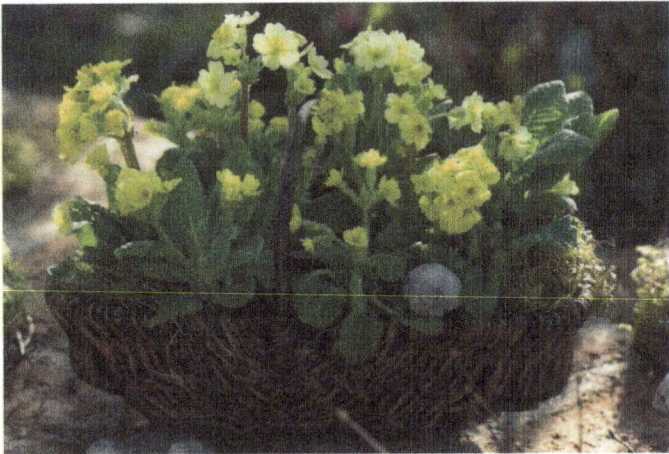

Losing Albert

Impossible to set down my feelings
These, the blackest days of my life.
My beautiful, loving, young husband
Gone from me.
He has for twenty years been my rock,
My dearest partner and lover.
Without him the world seems empty,
Bleak.
For the sake of our children
I have tried to cope with the horror
Of what has happened
But day after day has seen me
So devastated that my doctors insisted
Total rest was essential.

How could this have happened?
Why did I not realise the deterioration
Of his health?
Why did I not see that the entertainment
He constantly planned for me
And for our children
Was taking its toll on his body?
That, and his determination to see
That the vast amount of improvements
He had made at Windsor Castle,
Balmoral and Buckingham Palace
Were finished to his standard
All of it, draining his energy away.

I blame myself for being self-centred
And not devoting myself to his needs,
Now it is too late.
How to manage without him?
His loss, the funeral,
All an agonising nightmare.

Not until I return to our beloved Osborne
In our family home filled with memories
There, surrounded by what he achieved,
A place alive with his presence
Can any shred of normality be resumed.

.....

Footnote: Prince Albert's attendants were the first to recognise
that he was seriously unwell and working too hard.
They had noted that on arrival at Balmoral he had
checked that the farm buildings and offices were as
he had outlined, the gardens were in order and that a
new dairy had been installed, but always he found
further problems which must be dealt with.

Victoria now became increasingly aware also of his
ill health and the news that King Pedro of Portugal
and his brother had caught typhoid, created further
anxiety. To add to this, the knowledge that the
Prince of Wales had been involved in a scandal was
the last straw. Dr Jenner and his doctors now
acknowledged that the Prince was very ill, that
typhoid fever had taken over and they knew the end
was near.

For Victoria, the thought of she and Albert being
separated was unbelievable. Escorted from the
room after the final kiss on his brow, she attempted
to hold herself upright and held her head high, until
at last she was alone and allowed to grieve at the
loss of her beloved.

John Brown

Once again I have been dealt
The cruellest of blows.
A widow at forty-two with nine children
The loss of my dear husband
Was a hard cross to bear.
Now, when I had at last found
Someone else I could trust and admire,
Someone who was not afraid to question
My wishes, knowing that I could rely
On his integrity to criticise
With the best intentions,
Someone, who was never subservient,
Now, I am once again left bereft
And lonely without the support
And friendship of someone close to me.

I am well aware of the gossip
Surging through newspapers
And indeed through my own family
Who seemed always to resent
Our friendship,
Seeing in it something scurrilous
Or degrading
John Brown at all times showed me
Kindness and respect
On occasion even reprimanding
My own children for the ill-mannered way
In which they spoke to me.

His loss has left me once again devastated
And alone. Over the years,
I ensured that he was aware
Of my gratitude by creating
Two special awards in his name.

One, A Faithfull Servant Medal,
Two, a Devoted Service Medal.
Following his death I have had a life-size statue
Placed in the grounds of Balmoral.
He is not forgotten.

.....

Footnote: Born in Crathie, Scotland in 1826. John Brown was a ghillie, (outside worker) at Balmoral when the lease was first signed by Albert and Victoria and later bought.

The Royal children were indeed angry at the liaison. They privately referred to him as 'Mama's lover', or the Queen's 'stallion'. Rumours, as to the depth of the friendship, abound. The wife of Henry Ponsonby, the Queen's Private Secretary was told by her friend, sister of the Rev. Norman Macleod that on his deathbed the minister said that he had once married the Queen and John Brown, afterwards regretting it.

It was even said that an elderly American lady had told one of the German princes that she was a daughter of the union, but none of these rumours are proven and doctors said, following post-mortem examinations it was almost impossible for the Queen to have borne another child at the time stated.

Another rumour said that a historian found details of the secret wedding and showed it to the Queen Mother, who immediately, without comment, burned it.

General opinion seemed to be that Victoria's own respect for the dignity of the monarchy would have made any of circulating ideas out of the question.

Sadly, the Queen's children, now grown up, refused to address Brown, except as a servant.

The Prince of Wales refused to go to Abergeldie, saying that John Brown interfered with the shooting and he would not have this interfered with by a hired ghillie. The Queen heard this and was very angry, indeed!

On the one occasion when Prince Bertie was leaving for India, to everyone's surprise, Bertie put out his hand to Brown and when Brown said, 'God bless your Royal Highness and bring you safely back', the Queen burst into tears.

Everyone thought this was because her son was leaving - others knew, it was because, just for once, Bertie had been unusually polite!!

My Munshi

I am fortunate that so often
When another void has occurred in my life
Someone has appeared to carry me through
The darkest days.
As Empress of India, anxious to show my interest
And my deep regret at never having visited
Their country, I attended an exhibition in London
Demonstrating their art at weaving.
It was impressive and I asked their Superintendent
To recruit two members of his group
Who would be prepared to remain in Britain for a year
To act as servants at my Golden Jubilee.
Abdul Karim was one of those selected.

Later I learned from him that his father
Was a hospital assistant at a gaol
And after training as a clerk for several years
Abdul left his post to join his father.
There he had learned of the expedition of weavers
Going to Britain and asked to be included.
He was one of the two chosen to be schooled
In British manners and our language
And, at the close of the exhibition,
Sent to Windsor Castle.

I have never forgotten that first morning
When the two men served my breakfast…
The first thing they both did
Was kiss my feet!
When it was time for them to return home
I asked that Abdul should remain
As he had already acquainted me
With a few words of Hindustani and Urdu

This was invaluable when I was required
To meet and greet the Maharani
Of Chimnalsai of Barde.
Anxious to learn more of these languages
I appointed him as my munshi, i.e. teacher,
And arranged that he should have additional
Tuition in the English language.
Much, I might add, to the disgust of my children.

I fear they have been so privileged
That they cannot comprehend the leaps
Which have to be made by others
Who have experienced the poverty
Inherent in countries such as India.
I am hopeful that their distastefulness
Is not based on the colour of Abdul's skin.
They are old enough now to realise
That as monarch, my duties and my concern
Must be for the people in all my realms,
Regardless of colour and creed.

We were able, as Abdul's education developed
To have quite wide ranging discussions.
After a time I put him in charge of the Indian servants
And made him responsible for their accounts.
On occasions I deliberately placed him
In the company of gentry,
Causing jealousy and discontent amongst
The Royal Household.
At Balmoral he was given John Brown's room
And at Osborne he was at first assigned
To my physician's room and private sitting room.
Later I ensured Abdul had a house where,
When his mother visited, they could meet in private.

My physician was shocked when asked to see Abdul
And treat a nasty boil on his neck.
However, he knew better than to deny my request

And the matter was dealt with.
To Sir James Reid's amazement I visited Abdul daily
In his room, taking lessons, signing my boxes
Often examining his neck and shaking his pillows.
To me, he was just a boy.
A boy in a different world, trying to improve himself.
Yes, I praised him. He was good, gentle, clever,
Refined and pious. I determined to see
That he was taken care of in the future.
The painting I ordered of him, is a joy.
In the years to come people will admire the young
And handsome Indian. Hopefully by then,
Racism will be a thing of the past.

…..

Footnote: Queen Victoria gave the Munshi three houses… in Balmoral, Windsor and Osborne. She ordered that a plot of land be given to him in India. Abdul Karim was the last person to close the Queen's casket when she lay in state in Osborne, before transference to the mainland.

After the funeral, King Edward VII, Bertie, gave directions that the Munshi must now return home. He did so, to a wife and mother. The King also ordered that all correspondence between his mother and the Munshi be examined and destroyed. Reputedly, some letters were signed, 'Your truly devoted and loving mother'.

Dear, Desolate, Osborne

It was at first, our beautiful home
Bursting with family life.
Now, without Albert and my children
It is a place of loneliness.

Four sons and five daughters,
I surely had every right
To believe that one would have remained
Here with me?
Certainly I thought Beatrice
Would have been my constant companion
During these years.
But her meeting with Henri of Battenburg
Marked a turning point.
She told me their love was mutual
And couldn't be denied.

Down the years I have given much time
And thought to my children's partners
In marriage.
It was worth the effort.
Now their children reap the benefits,
As royal descendants
With the likelihood of themselves
Creating future kings, queens, princes
And princesses.

Bertie, although lacking in his father's
Intelligence and knowledge,
At last shows a greater aptitude
For future kingship.
My first meeting with Alexandra of Denmark
Led me to believe her unsuitable.
I was wrong! She is quiet and caring,
Always elegant, a perfect future queen.

Sadly, Leo died as a result of the sickness
He has carried since birth.
His health a constant source of worry.
I had hoped he would not marry,
But he met Helen of Waldek and Pyrment
And a wedding was not to be refused.
Albert always said the boy should live
As normal a life as possible.
He would be pleased that,
For however short a time,
Leo loved and was loved by a young lady
Of his choosing.

My own ladies are a great comfort to me.
Whenever the weather permits
One of them accompanies me in the carriage.
We ride along the lanes of the estate
And those around Barton manor,
The farm which, after a great deal of persistence,
Albert and I were eventually able to buy.
The glimpses of the sea and the yachts
Are delightful.
Our tenants run out of their cottages,
To wave and smile at our passing.
Always, I have attended to their welfare
I realise this is their way of showing
Their appreciation

…..

Footnote: Whilst abroad, Leo bumped his knee on a staircase
and the internal bleeding could not be staunched.
He died in his 31st year.

Princess Beatrice was appointed Lord Lieutenant of
the Isle of Wight and, as her mother got older,
endeavoured to spend as much time as possible with
her. Beatrice had three sons and one daughter.

My Last Message

I am tired, so very tired
The eyes of my ladies say it all,
Reveal that they are thinking
My time is drawing to its close.
I have only one regret
Which has over-shadowed these last years
My dearest taken from me
Whilst we were still so young,
So happy together.

People whisper to each other.
Smile when I pore over charts
Defining the royal houses of Europe,
They are no longer smiling.
I have achieved my ambition
And now, embedded in those palaces
Carrying our blood, our seed,
Albert and I will live on in their dynasties.
Making me truly,
The Grandmother of Europe.

My farewells to the palaces and to the churches
Crathie and Whippingham, have been made.
Here in my beloved Osborne,
I feel always the comforting presence of Albert
Reliving the joy of those surprises
Planned for my benefit,
Surrounding myself in his creations.

My physician knows all that must travel with me,
Will place them in private in the casket
Leaving my dear Munshi, like a son to me,
To close the lid and wish me 'God speed'.
All is prepared…

The Royal family now attended to see the body for the last time. In the presence of the new King, the coffin was sealed, covered with a white pall and carried by a party of sailors to the dining room, which had been prepared as a chapel. There soldiers mounted guard.

The funeral cortege was to leave through the entrance which had, during Victoria's lifetime, become known as the Sovereign's Gate and holds that title to this day.

Many people gathered at the roadside to see the gun carriage bearing the coffin, as it was drawn by the Royal Horse Artillery regiment to Trinity Pier. There it was placed on the yacht Alberta. Following were three other yachts bearing the Royals and their suites.

As the yachts approached Southsea, vast crowds lined the shore. Throughout the crossing, miles of warships could be heard firing their minute guns

For her Beloved Osborne, it was without doubt, a very fitting ending for a much admired Queen.

.....

Footnote: As her children grew older, Victoria spent a great deal of time trying to ensure that they met from all over Europe many Royal families and, in fact, married many of their members!!

Victoria, Grandmother of Europe

Behind her,
Years of maternal domination
A Queen now,
Her young, loving husband
Hand-picked and handsome
Conceiving children a delight,
Bearing them a necessity.

Bereft and widowed at forty-two
Determined still to breed
A unique elite.
Her nine children to provide the seed,
Planned with precision
To feed royal dynasties.

Unfailing in her duty as Queen
Her offspring spread across Europe
With forcefulness and insistence
Ensuring it must take precedence.
The result was,
To quote her favourite phrase,
'Satisfying… very satisfying.'

.....

Osborne House

The Children of Queen Victoria

Queen Victoria was the only child of Edward, Duke of Kent, fourth son of King George III and a younger brother of King George IV and King William IV. She was born in 1819, succeeded her uncle, King William IV, in 1837, and in 1840 married her cousin, Prince Albert of Saxe-Coburg, who died at Windsor in 1861. They had nine children:

1. *Princess Victoria (the Princess Royal) (1840-1901), mother of Kaiser Wilhelm II*
2. *King Edward VII (1841-1910)*
3. *Princess Alice (1843-1878)*
4. *Prince Alfred, Admiral of the Fleet the Duke of Edinburgh (1844-1900)*
5. *Princess Helena (1846-1923)*
6. *Princess Louise (1848-1939)*
7. *Prince Arthur, Field Marshal the Duke of Connaught (1850-1942)*
8. *Prince Leopold, Duke of Albany (1853-1884)*
9. *Princess Beatrice (1857-1944)*

HER MAJESTY'S DINNER
OSBORNE HOUSE
Christmas Day 1895

Puree of celery a la
crème
Cream of rise a
l'Indienne
Puree of pheasant a la
Chasseur
Soles frites
Sauce aux anchois

Woodcocks a la Robert
Quenelles of fowls a
l'essence
Salmis of widgeon a la
Bigamade
Border of rice garnished
with
A puree of pheasant

Filet de boeuf
Roast turkey a la
Perignon
Roast goose a L'Anglaise
Faisans
Gelinottes

Plum pudding
Mince pies a l'Anglaise
Puddings a la Gotha
Pudding de Cabinet
Tourte de pommes a la
Cobourg

… …

On the Sideboard

Boar's head
Baron of beef
Woodcock pie

Wines
Sherry or Amontillado
Dry white wines
Champagne & Moselle
Burgundy & Bordeaux
Malmsey-Madeira
Liqueurs
Port, Sherry, Claret
(Balmoral whisky &
Apollinaris for the use
of Her Majesty, who
takes nothing else)

HER MAJESTY'S DINNER
OSBORNE HOUSE
Christmas Day 1896

Potages
La Tete de Veau En
Torte. Aux trios raciness
Poissons
Le Turbot bouilli sauce
hollandaise
Les Filets de soles frits
Entrée
Les Kromeskys a la
Toulouse
Releves
Les Dindes roties a la
Chipolata
Chine of Pork
Rt. Sirloin of Beef Plum
Pudding
Entremets
Les Asperges sauce
mousseline
Mince Pies
Le Pain de riz a la cintra

Side Table

... ...

Baron of Beef Woodcock
Pie Brawn
Wild Boar's Head Game
Pie

On the Sideboard

Boar's head
Baron of beef
Woodcock pie

Wines

Sherry or Amontillado
Dry white wines
Champagne & Moselle
Burgundy & Bordeaux
Malmsey-Madeira
Liqueurs
Port, Sherry, Claret
(Balmoral whisky &
Apollinaris for the use of
Her Majesty, who takes
nothing else.)

Lightning Source UK Ltd.
Milton Keynes UK
UKOW06f0624270116

267203UK00011B/54/P